ESSENTIAL
KANBAN
CONDENSED

DAVID J ANDERSON   ANDY CARMICHAEL

LeanKanban
UNIVERSITY
P R E S S
SEATTLE, WA

LeanKanban
UNIVERSITY
P R E S S

Library of Congress Cataloging in Publication Data

Names: Anderson, David J., 1967– | Carmichael, Andy.
Title: Essential Kanban condensed / David J Anderson [and] Andy Carmichael.
Description: First edition. | [Seattle, Washington] : Lean Kanban University Press, 2016. | Series: [Essential Kanban] ; [2] | Includes bibliographical references and index.
Identifiers: ISBN 978-0-9845214-2-5
Subjects: LCSH: Just-in-time systems. | Lean manufacturing. | Production management. | Computer software—Development—Management.
Classification: LCC TS157.4 .A544 2016 | DDC 658.51—dc23

 Visit edu.leankanban.com for a list of accredited Kanban classes, coaches, and trainers, and information about becoming a Kanban coach or trainer.

 Visit services.leankanban.com or email sales@leankanban.com for information regarding private training or consulting for your organization.

Contents

Foreword

Kanban is a method that shows us how our work works.

It brings us a shared understanding of the work we do, including the rules by which we do the work, how much we can handle at a time, and how well we deliver work to our internal and external customers.

Once we achieve this understanding, we can start to improve. We can become more predictable and work at a more sustainable pace. Communication and collaboration goes up. So does quality. The people doing the work can act more independently because they develop an innate understanding of risk management.

We can also use Kanban to achieve better alignment across our entire enterprise, meaning that sweeping strategic goals can be achieved.

Kanban's focus on managed commitment and a balanced flow of work leads to greater agility. If market conditions change or issues with dependencies arise, Kanban provides the ability to change course quickly. This is why we call it the Alternative Path to Agility.

In 2011, Lean Kanban University set out to establish a standard of quality for the way Kanban is taught and practiced. Today we have a curriculum of Kanban training at all levels, which includes professional development programs as well as community events and resources. A global network of LKU trainers and coaches assures the quality and consistency of Kanban and the ongoing evolution of this body of knowledge.

This short book covers core concepts as we understand Kanban. It is based on the contributions of a vibrant global community committed to Kanban and to doing all that it can to improve the world of work.

Janice Linden-Reed
President, Lean Kanban, Inc.

Preface

This book provides a distillation of Kanban: the "essence" of what it is and how it can be used. It covers a lot of ground in just a few short pages, which in many cases narrows the scope, so as only to introduce a topic rather than to explain it fully. Our goal is to give you a brief overview in a format that might fit in your pocket—to introduce all the principal concepts and guidelines in Kanban—and also, in the final section, to point you to where you can find out more. We hope it provides quick access to the key concepts in Kanban, as well as encouragement to embark on, or to continue, a life-long journey of exploration and exploitation of these ideas.

The Kanban Method—Kanban as we will generally refer to it—is concerned with the design, management, and improvement of flow systems for knowledge work. These are systems in which intangible work items move through different stages, eventually resulting in value to their customers. Since these work items can be very different between systems (for example, a "to do" item for a small administration team, a new feature in software product development, or one of many "initiatives" overseen by a portfolio management group), the nature of different Kanban implementations also varies widely. This book aims to express the common values, principles, and practices that underlie the approach, and to provide a common vocabulary for those applying the method. To that end, we have included an extensive Kanban Glossary that defines the terms we use and recommend for use in the Kanban community.

Our goal is to capture Kanban's essence as briefly as possible. As a result, this book is short on detail, advice, choices, and specific examples—for these, see the original book on the Kanban Method,

David Anderson's *Kanban: Successful Evolutionary Change for Your Technology Business* (Blue Hole Press, 2010).

We first discussed the need for this Kanban guide back in 2013, when there were only a few books available on the method other than David's own. The main (unreliable) sources that people were using to answer the question "What is Kanban?" were incomplete add-ons from tool vendors and marketing literature promoting alternatives. Much progress was being made on the method within a relatively small community attending workshops and conferences, and although Kanban's popularity was growing rapidly in the wider user community, many Kanban implementations remained quite shallow in their adoption of the emerging ideas. In an attempt to remedy that, this book introduces all of Kanban's essential elements so that there can be a shared understanding of the method among those who use and discuss it. We hope it inspires a desire to study the method in greater depth for those leading change.

Caricatures of the method continue to abound: "Scrum without timeboxes," "Suitable for the helpdesk, but not for development," "A good replacement for a to-do list," "A change method for small changes," "A Waterfall rather than Agile method," "Only has three rules, so does not provide guidance," "A method without a process." These all are comments that you may have heard or read if you browse the critics' blogs and papers. We aim to remove some of the misinformation about the method so you can judge for yourself whether it is useful.

According to surveys of Agile organizations, the Kanban Method is widely used, either as the main process or in conjunction with another, such as Scrum. Like all similar reporting, what people are actually using may differ greatly from the definition of the method they name, so we don't really know if it is being used effectively; what we do know is that there are a lot of management teams out there that need to know more about what the Kanban Method means. We offer this book as the starting point for such a learning journey.

David J Anderson, Seattle, WA
Andy Carmichael, Southampton, UK

Conventions

The Glossary contains the definitions of a number of terms that are commonly used in Kanban. At least the first time a Glossary term appears in the text it is in boldface, e.g., **Delivery Rate**.

Kanban (the word) appears many times in this book, but readers will notice it is not always capitalized. The Kanban Method was so named in 2007 following presentations of the management approach that David had been using at Microsoft (Anderson, 2005) and Corbis, and the formation of a community around these and similar ideas. The Kanban Method, Kanban, or Kanban community is always capitalized in the text, when used in this sense.

However the Japanese word "kanban" (meaning "sign," "signal card," "tally," or "large visual board") has been used in the context of process definition since at least the 1960s, when Toyota named the systems they had been using to limit **work in progress** in their manufacturing plants "**kanban systems**" (Shimokawa, 2009). Such systems were just one of the many threads of inspiration behind the Kanban Method, although it is how the name for the method arose. Thus kanban is *not* capitalized in this text when referring to kanban systems, to **kanbans** (the physical cards or virtual signals that kanban systems use to control work in progress), or to **kanban boards**.

The plural of kanban in Japanese is "kanban"; however, we use the plural "kanbans" in this English text.

What is Kanban?

Kanban is a method for defining, managing, and improving **services** that deliver **knowledge work**, such as professional services, creative endeavors, and the design of both physical and software products. It may be characterized as a "start from what you do now" method—a catalyst for rapid and focused change within organizations—that reduces resistance to beneficial change in line with the organization's goals.

The Kanban Method is based on making visible what is otherwise intangible knowledge work, to ensure that the service works on the right amount of work—work that is requested and needed by the customer and that the service has the capability to deliver. To do this, we use a **kanban system**—a delivery **flow system** that limits the amount of **work in progress** (WiP) by using visual signals.

The signaling mechanisms, sometimes referred to as **kanbans,**[1] are displayed on **kanban boards** and represent **WiP Limits**, which prevent too much or too little work entering the system, thereby improving the flow of value to customers. The WiP Limit **policies** create a **pull system**: Work is "pulled" into the system when other work is completed and capacity becomes available, rather than "pushed" into it when new work is demanded.

Kanban focuses on the delivery of **services** by an organization—one or more people collaborating to produce (usually intangible) work products. A **service** has a customer, who requests the work or whose needs are identified, and who accepts or acknowledges delivery of the completed work. Even where there is a physical product from services, value resides less in the item itself and more in its informational content (the software, in the most general sense).

Kanban Values

The Kanban Method is values led. It is motivated by the belief that respecting all of the individuals who contribute to a collaborative enterprise is necessary, not only for the success of the venture, but for it to be worthwhile at all.

Kanban's values may be summed up in that single word, "respect." However, it is useful to expand this into a set of nine values[2] (including respect) that encapsulates why the principles and practices of Kanban exist (Figure 1).

Transparency The belief that sharing information openly improves the flow of business value. Using clear and straightforward vocabulary is part of this value.

Figure 1 Kanban's Values

Balance   The understanding that different aspects, viewpoints, and capabilities all must be balanced for effectiveness. Some aspects (such as demand and capability) will cause breakdown if they are out of balance for an extended period.

Collaboration   Working together. The Kanban Method was formulated to improve the way people work together, so collaboration is at its heart.

Customer Focus   Knowing the goal for the system. Every kanban system flows to a point of realizing value—when customers receive a required item or service. Customers in this context are external to the service, but may be internal or external to the organization as a whole. The customers and the value they receive is the natural point of focus in Kanban.

Flow   The realization that work is a *flow* of value, whether continuous or episodic. Seeing flow is an essential starting point in using Kanban.

Leadership   The ability to inspire others to action through example, words, and reflection. Most organizations have some degree of hierarchical structure, but in Kanban leadership is needed at all levels to achieve value delivery and improvement.

Understanding   Primarily self-knowledge (both of the individual and of the organization) in order to move forward. Kanban is an improvement method, and knowing the starting point is foundational.

Agreement   The commitment to move together toward goals, respecting—and where possible, accommodating—differences of opinion or approach. This is not management by consensus, but a dynamic co-commitment to improvement.

Respect Valuing, understanding, and showing consideration for people. Appropriately at the foot of this list, it is the foundation on which the other values rest.

These values embody the motivations of Kanban in seeking to improve services delivered by collaborating teams. The method cannot be applied faithfully without embracing them.

Kanban Agendas

It might be considered that Kanban, as a "start with what you do now" method, comes with no agenda as to the type or purpose of the change it initiates. In fact, Kanban recognizes three **agendas**—three compelling calls to action based on organizational need:

1. *The Sustainability Agenda* is about finding a sustainable pace and improving focus.

2. *The Service Orientation Agenda* focuses attention on performance and customer satisfaction.

3. *The Survivability Agenda* is concerned with staying competitive and adaptive.

The Sustainability Agenda looks inward to the organization. Its goal is to build

Figure 2 Kanban's agendas

services that are not overburdened with work, but that balance demand with capability, thereby improving the performance of services with regard to customer satisfaction, staff engagement and collaboration, and cost. It is a natural starting point for change because, in situations where demand outstrips capability, making intangible work visible and reducing overburdening in the servicing of the work is likely to have an immediate positive impact on the amount of work completed, the time needed to complete work items, and staff morale.

The Service Orientation Agenda looks outward from the organization's purpose to its customers. It should be the clearest and most explicit agenda for all organizations. The goal is to provide services to customers that are fit for purpose—that meet and exceed customers' needs and expectations. This should be viewed as transcending sub-goals such as profitability or returning value to shareholders, which ultimately are merely means to that end. When everyone in the organization—every department and every service—focuses on providing service to their customers, the organization itself will achieve outstanding results. Kanban is about delivering services and improving them, and the Service Orientation Agenda is a key to its success.

The Survivability Agenda looks forward to the future. It seeks to ensure that an organization survives and thrives in times of significant change. The pace of change and the emergence of disruptors in all major markets means that no organization can assume current processes and technology will suffice for even a few years into the future. Kanban's evolutionary approach to change—with its focus on safe-to-fail, continuous improvement; encouraging diversity in processes and technology; and respect and engagement for all stakeholders involved—is an appropriate response to this constant challenge.

The Foundational Principles of Kanban

There are six foundational principles of Kanban, which may be divided into two groups: the change management principles and the service delivery principles (Figure 3).

Change Management Principles

Your organization is a network of individuals, psychologically and sociologically wired to resist change. Kanban acknowledges these human aspects with three *change management principles*:

1. Start with what you do now:

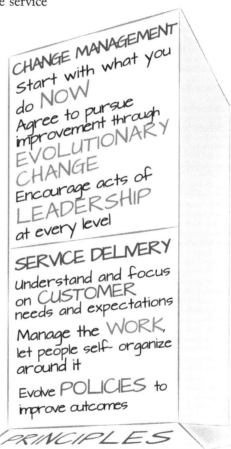

Figure 3 Kanban's principles

- understanding current processes, as they are actually practiced and
- respecting existing roles, responsibilities, and job titles.

2. Agree to pursue improvement through evolutionary change.

3. Encourage acts of leadership at every level—from the individual contributor to senior management.

There are two key reasons that "starting from here" is a good idea. The first is that minimizing resistance to change by respecting current practice and practitioners is crucial to engaging everyone in meeting the challenges of the future. The second is that the current processes, along with their obvious deficiencies, contain wisdom and resilience that even those working with them may not fully appreciate. Since change is essential, we should not impose solutions from different contexts, but instead agree to pursue evolutionary improvement across all levels of the organization. Starting from current practice establishes the baseline of performance and effectiveness from which future changes can be assessed.

Service Delivery Principles

Any sizable organization is an ecosystem of interdependent services. Kanban acknowledges this with three *service delivery principles*, applicable not just to one service but to the whole network:

1. Understand and focus on your customers' needs and expectations.

2. Manage the work; let people self-organize around it.

3. Evolve policies to improve customer and business outcomes.

These principles align closely with the service orientation agenda and the value of customer focus. When the work itself and the flow of value to customers that it represents are not clearly visible, organizations often focus instead on what *is* visible, the people working on the service. Are they always busy? Are they skilled enough? Could they work harder? The customer and the work items that represent value to the customer receive less attention. What these principles stress is that the focus must move back to the consumers of the service and value they receive from it.

Describing Flow Systems

Kanban is used to define, manage, and improve systems that deliver services of value to customers. As Kanban is applied to knowledge work, where the deliveries consist of information in various forms rather than physical items, the processes can be defined as a series of knowledge-discovery steps and their associated **policies**, made visible in a **kanban board** such as the one in Figure 4.

The board depicts a flow system in which work items flow through various stages of a process, ordered from left to right.

Several conditions must exist for this flow system to be a **kanban system**. First, there must be signals (usually visual signals) to limit **work in progress (WiP)**. In this case, the signals derive from the combination of the **cards**, the displayed **Work in Progress Limits** (in the rectangles at the head of the columns), and the column that represents the **activity**. In addition, **kanban systems** must have identified **commitment** and **delivery** points.

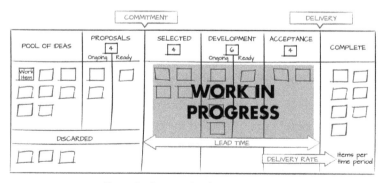

Figure 4 An example of a kanban board

The commitment is an explicit or tacit agreement between customer and service that:

1. the customer wants an item and will take delivery of it, and
2. the service will produce it and deliver it to the customer.

Before the commitment point there may be a set of outstanding requests (or a pool of ideas), which may or may not be selected, and a process whose purpose is selecting items from these **options**. Kanban applied to processes prior to the commitment point is sometimes referred to as **Discovery Kanban**.[3] The **delivery point** is where items are considered complete.

The time that an item is in process between the commitment and delivery points is referred to as the item's **Lead Time** (or **System Lead Time**). **Customer Lead Time** may be different—it is the time a customer waits for the item (typically from request to receipt). The fact that a distinction is made between the creation, or arrival, of a request and the commitment to fulfill the request is important; it is referred to as **deferred commitment**. Anomalies in the definition of system lead time and customer lead time occur for two reasons: the customer has not agreed to adopt a pull system and still pushes work for delivery regardless of capacity or capability to process it; the service delivery is internal to a wider network of services and not directly coupled to the originating customer request, hence the internal requesting "customer" has already committed to the work and the receiving service has no option other than to make their best effort to process it in a timely manner.

The collection of items that are within the system under consideration at any point in time, as well as the count of the number of these items, is known as the **Work in Progress** or **WiP**.

The rate at which items are delivered is known as the **Delivery Rate**. This is calculated from the reciprocal of the time between the latest delivery and the previous one or, for an average Delivery Rate over a given period, by dividing the number of deliveries by the length of the time period.

Little's Law

In a flow system that is not trending[4] (and in which all items that are selected are delivered) there is a simple relationship between the *averages* of these metrics over a specific period. It is known as Little's Law:[5]

$$\overline{Delivery\ Rate} = \frac{\overline{WiP}}{\overline{Lead\ Time}}$$

where the overline denotes arithmetic mean.

We may wish to use Little's Law to examine the flow metrics of other parts of a **kanban system**—not just between the commitment and delivery points—in which case, rather than **Lead Time** we use **Time in Process** or **TiP**[6] for the period an item is in the process under consideration. More specific terms such as Time in Development, Time in Test, Time in System (synonymous with **System Lead Time**) or Time in Queue may also be used.

The term **Throughput** is used instead of **Delivery Rate** if the end of the process under consideration is not the **delivery point**.[7]

Here is an alternative formulation of Little's Law using these terms:

$$\overline{Throughput} = \frac{\overline{WiP}}{\overline{TiP}}$$

Little's Law many be demonstrated graphically on a **Cumulative Flow Diagram**, as shown in Figure 5, which plots the cumulative number of items arriving and departing from a system.

The Approximate Average Lead Time (Approx Av. LT) and the Approximate Average WiP (Approx Av. WiP) are marked on the diagram. The gradient of the hypotenuse of the marked triangle is the Average Delivery Rate over this period and, in line with Little's Law, it can be seen to be:

$$\frac{Approx\ Av.\ WiP}{Approx\ Av.\ LT}$$

The actual averages for Lead Time and WiP have to be calculated from individual items, but in non-trending systems they will approximate to these values.

Little's Law provides an important insight into kanban systems: in order to optimize the **Lead Time** for work items, we must limit the **Work in Progress**. This is one of the General Practices of Kanban.

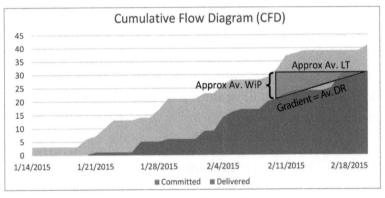

Figure 5   A Cumulative Flow Diagram

The General Practices of Kanban

The General Practices of Kanban define essential activities for those managing kanban systems (Figure 6). There are six of them.

1. Visualize.
2. Limit work in progress.
3. Manage flow.
4. Make policies explicit.
5. Implement feedback loops.
6. Improve collaboratively, evolve experimentally.

These practices all involve:

- *seeing* the work and the policies that determine how it is processed; then
- *improving* the process in an evolutionary fashion —keeping and amplifying useful change and learning from and reversing or dampening ineffective change.

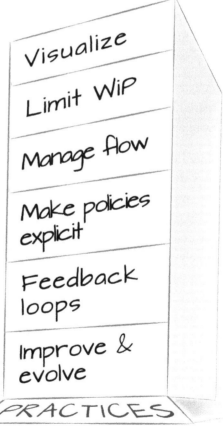

Figure 6 Kanban's practices

Let's look at each of the general practices in more detail.

Visualize

A **kanban board** such as in the diagram in Figure 4 (on page 13) is one, though not the only, way to visualize work and the process it goes through. For it to be a **kanban system** rather than simply a flow system, the commitment and delivery points must be defined, and WiP Limits must be displayed to limit the work in progress at each stage between these points. The act of making work and policies visible—whether on a wall board, in electronic displays, or other means—is the result of an important journey of collaboration to understand the current system and find potential areas for improvement.

Policies, too, are important to visualize; for example, by placing summaries between columns of what must be done before items move from one column to the next.

Board design varies greatly among kanban systems, depending on how they are used (see, for example, the *Kanbanraum* in Figure 6). The method does not constrain how to design them. Software tools developed to support Kanban may introduce practical constraints—for example, the common pattern of a two-dimensional grid with panels displaying information about each work item. The columns represent steps in a process, and some of the columns have horizontal partitions (called **swimlanes**, if they cross two or more columns) to distinguish **states** of items within the steps. However it is interesting to note that teams designing physical boards, without such constraints, often find other creative ways to display information of importance to them, including connections to boards belonging to other services.

Figure 6 The "Kanbanraum" at Visotech uses many different kinds of visualizations to see the work, the type of work, and the effort.[8]

Design of the card or panel that describes the work item is another essential aspect of visualization. It is also vital to highlight visually when items are blocked by dependencies on other services or for other reasons.

Limit Work in Progress

Introducing and respecting limits on **WiP** changes a "push" system into a "pull" system, in which new items are not started until work is completed (or on rarer occasions, **aborted**). Having too much partially complete work is wasteful and expensive and, crucially, it lengthens lead times, preventing the organization from being responsive to their customers and to changing circumstances and opportunities.

Observing, limiting, and then optimizing the amount of work in progress is essential to success with Kanban (Figure 7), as it results in improved lead time for services, improved quality, and a higher rate of deliveries.[9]

By contrast, ineffective management behavior focuses on maximizing the usage of people and resources by trying to ensure that everyone is "busy" with a ready supply of work so that no idle time occurs.[10] As a result, people may feel overwhelmed with the amount they have to do and accept only tasks they have been explicitly instructed to carry out; they may lose sight of the service they provide and how it contributes to the overall goals of the organization and its customers.

Figure 7   Limiting WiP provokes discussion and improvement.
(from the cover of [Anderson, 2010])

The General Practices of Kanban

Manage Flow

The flow of work in a kanban system should maximize the delivery of value, minimize lead times, and be as smooth (i.e. predictable) as possible. These are sometimes conflicting goals and, since the deliverables are usually complex, empirical control through transparency, inspection, and adaption is required. Bottlenecks, where flow is constrained by one particular sub-process, and blockers, where there are dependencies on other services, are important to take note of and manage.

A key to understanding and maximizing the flow of value is the **cost of delay (CoD)** of work items. The amount of an item's value that is lost by delaying its implementation by a specified period of time is referred to as the **delay cost**, and the *rate* at which the value changes (the delay cost per time period) is referred to as the **urgency** or the **cost of delay**. In general, both delay cost and urgency vary with the length of the delay. Kanban uses four archetypes to characterize how the value of items changes with delay: expedite, fixed date, standard, and intangible (Figure 8).

These archetypes may be used to assist in ordering work items, or they may define different **classes of service**, where different policies are applied to different types of work.[11]

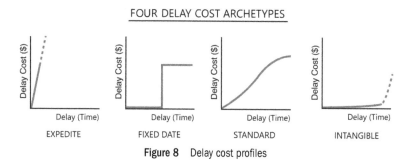

FOUR DELAY COST ARCHETYPES

EXPEDITE   FIXED DATE   STANDARD   INTANGIBLE

Figure 8   Delay cost profiles

The relationship with the consumers of the service, the customers, is a key aspect of managing flow. Lead Time, especially Customer Lead Time, is a key metric for customers, though many other aspects are important, including: Delivery Rate, defect rate (and other quality measures), and predictability of supply. Different service levels such as the following may be defined for kanban systems to guide this.

- *Service Level Expectation* what the customer expects
- *Service Level Capability* what the system can deliver
- *Service Level Agreement* what is agreed with the customer
- *Service Fitness Threshold* the service level below which the service delivery is unacceptable to the customer

Make Policies Explicit

Explicit policies are a way of articulating and defining a process that goes beyond the workflow definition. A process expressed as workflow *and* policies creates constraints on action, is empowering within the constraints, and results in emergent characteristics that can be tuned by experiment. The process policies need to be sparse, simple, well-defined, visible, always applied, and readily changeable by those providing the service. Note that "always applied" and "readily changeable" go together. Setting WiP limits, and then never challenging, changing, or breaking the limits to see whether different limits in differing circumstances improve outcomes, would be a poor application of this practice.

The behavior of complex systems, though they may be guided by simple policies, is not possible to predict. Policies that may seem intuitively obvious (for example, "the sooner you start, the sooner you'll finish") often produce counterintuitive results. For this reason, it is a core practice to make explicit the policies that apply to services and for there to be a visible and straightforward mechanism

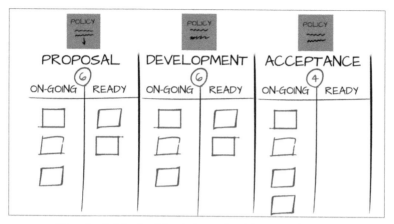

Figure 9   Policies for different stages of work (above each column)

to question and change policies when they are considered counter-productive or are found not to be applied.

WiP Limits are one type of policy; others include capacity allocation and balancing, the "Definition of Done," or other policies for work items exiting the stages of a process (see Figure 9). **Replenishment** policies for selecting new work when capacity is available and using classes of service are additional policy examples.

Implement Feedback Loops

Feedback loops are an essential part of any controlled process and are especially important for evolutionary change. Improving feedback in all areas of the process is important, but it is particularly so in the following:

- strategy alignment
- operational coordination
- risk management
- service improvement

- replenishment
- flow
- customer deliveries

Kanban defines seven specific feedback opportunities, or **cadences**. Cadences are the cyclical meetings and reviews that drive evolutionary change and effective service delivery. "Cadence" may also refer to the time period between reviews—one workday or one month, for example. Choosing the right cadence is context dependent and it is crucial to good outcomes. Too-frequent reviews may compel changing things before seeing the effect of previous changes, but if they are not frequent enough, poor performance may persist longer than necessary.

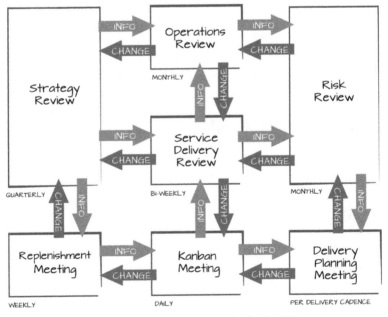

Figure 10 A set of cadences showing feedback loops

A scheme of seven cadences, depicted in Figure 10, shows suggested frequencies for the reviews in a typical enterprise or multiple-service context.

1. *Strategy Review*   This is for selection of the services to be provided and to define for this set of services the concept of "fit for purpose"; also for sensing how the external environment is changing in order to provide direction to the services.

2. *Operations Review*   This is to understand the balance between and across services, deploying resources to maximize the delivery of value aligned with customers' expectations.

3. *Risk Review*   This review is to understand and respond to the risks to effective delivery of services; for example, through **blocker clustering**.

4. *Service Delivery Review*   This is to examine and improve the effectiveness of a service (this and subsequent cadences apply to a single service).

5. *Replenishment Meeting*   This meeting is for moving items over the commitment point (and into the system) and to oversee the preparation of options for future selection.

6. *The Kanban Meeting*   This is the (usually) daily coordination, self-organization, and planning review for those collaborating to deliver the service. It often uses a "stand-up" format to encourage a short, energetic meeting with the focus on completing work items and unblocking issues.

7. *Delivery Planning Meeting*   This is to monitor and plan deliveries to customers.

Implementing the seven cadences does not imply adding seven new meetings to an organization's overhead, although the Replenishment and Kanban Meetings are considered a baseline in nearly all Kanban implementations. Initially, the agenda of each cadence should be part of existing meetings and adapted in context to fulfill their goals. On a smaller scale, a single meeting may cover more than one cadence.

The feedback loops in the cadence network diagram (Figure 10) show example information flow and requests for change between the reviews. These facilitate decision making at each level.

Improve Collaboratively, Evolve Experimentally

Kanban is fundamentally an improvement method. Often, transformation programs are started with the aim to change processes to a new, predefined approach. In contrast, Kanban starts from the organization as it is now and uses the Lean flow paradigm[12] (seeing work as a flow of value) to pursue continuous and incremental improvement. There is no endpoint of such change processes since perfection in an ever-changing **fitness landscape** is unattainable. Kanban harnesses an evolutionary process to allow beneficial change to occur within an organization, protecting it from another natural evolutionary process—extinction! Organizations cannot opt out of evolution: It either works for them or happens to them. But they can choose to encourage the change to occur from within, rather than finding it is unable to respond to existential threats from without. Kanban facilitates this.

The evolutionary process involves differentiation (copying with deliberate differences or mutations); selecting for fitness; and keeping and amplifying useful change while dampening or reversing ineffective change.[13]

It can be useful to employ models and the scientific method to validate or invalidate applying the models in context. Sometimes using empirical and pragmatic approaches is an appropriate way to find the greatest fitness for purpose within the current environment.

Introducing Kanban to Organizations

It is simple to start using Kanban: Recognize that your work involves a flow of value from the request for an item to its delivery to your customer; visualize the work and the process for delivering the work; then continually improve the process by applying the values, the principles, and the practices.[14]

All through this process you will be applying Kanban, even while the characteristics of your systems are barely different from your starting point. Clearly, this means that there are organizations applying Kanban that do not yet even have a **kanban system** (a system that limits work in progress with visual signals), or whose kanban systems have not yet matured, for example, to an effective balancing of demand with capability through feedback loops, or to optimal value delivery through **classes of service**.

Such systems may be referred to as **protokanban** systems because they are systems being transformed by Kanban, though not yet compliant with its general practices.[15] Protokanban systems can bring great benefit to organizations—for example, in making intangible work visible—but they should not be viewed as endpoints in process transformations.

For these reasons, the Kanban Method defines an approach for introducing Kanban (STATIK) and a test for assessing your progress with Kanban (the Litmus Test).

Systems Thinking Approach to Introducing Kanban (STATIK)

Systems Thinking[16] is a way of understanding how a system behaves as a whole rather than through analysis of isolated component parts. It is a key influence in defining the steps needed to introduce Kanban in an organization. The steps in this process are not necessarily sequential, but iterative—using learning from one step to inform and influence the others in a collaborative environment. The steps are as follows.

Step 0 Identify services.

For each service . . .

Step 1 Understand what makes the service fit for purpose for the customer.

Step 2 Understand sources of dissatisfaction with the current system.

Step 3 Analyze demand.

Step 4 Analyze capability.

Step 5 Model workflow.

Step 6 Discover classes of service.

Step 7 Design the kanban system.

Step 8 Socialize the system and board design and negotiate implementation.

STATIK is applicable to just one service. When more than one service has been set up, Kanban practices and cadences are applied to balance demand and flow across the multiple services and to continually improve. The emphasis on Systems Thinking here is important. If services are improved in isolation, this results in "sub-optimization." The system as a whole, with its goal of improving the flow of value to customers, must be considered. Sometimes this means that the first services to address with STATIK might be those that operate at a higher level and are delivering directly to customers, rather than internal services delivering within the organization.

In practice, the order of the steps in STATIK may vary, and it is normal to revisit steps in pursuit of further improvement.

The Kanban Litmus Test

The Kanban Litmus Test is designed to help organizations assess their progress with Kanban and suggest areas that may yield effective improvements. It consists of a series of four questions; the first questions are prerequisites for those that follow.

1. Has *management behavior* changed to enable Kanban?
2. Has the *customer interface* changed, in line with Kanban?
3. Has the *customer contract* changed, informed by Kanban?
4. Has your *service delivery business model* changed to exploit Kanban?

1. *Management Behavior*

An organization adopting Kanban needs managers who respect kanban system policies, embrace customer focus as a value, and manage work in line with the service delivery principles.

Ask these supplementary questions . . .

- Is management behavior consistent with Kanban's **deferred commitment, pull system** approach?

- Are **WiP** limits respected by management at the system level, not just at a personal level (such as per-person WiP limits to reduce multitasking)?
- Is customer focus always an understood reason for change?

2. *Customer Interface*

The services in the organization need true **kanban systems** with deferred commitment and a Replenishment Meeting to schedule, sequence, and select work. This provides a customer interface focused on maximizing the flow of value within the constraints of current capability.

Ask these supplementary questions . . .

- Is the approach to scheduling and selecting customer requests based on a pull system with limited work in progress?
- Are the commitment and delivery points clearly defined and are records of Lead Times and Delivery Rates available?
- Is there a regular Replenishment Meeting?

3. *Customer Contract*

The customer contract, whether a formal *service level agreement* or an understood *service level expectation*, should be based on measured performance of the service, such as Lead Times and Delivery Rates.

Ask these supplementary questions . . .

- Are commitments made to the customer based on the agreed or understood service levels (explicit *service level agreements* or *service level expectations*)?
- Are these levels based on probabilistic forecasting using the kanban system's observed Lead Times and Delivery Rates?

Introducing Kanban to Organizations

4. *Service Business Model*

In services with established kanban systems, improved value and risk management is possible, for example, through classes of service, capacity allocation, demand shaping, and differential pricing.

Ask these supplementary questions . . .

- Does the service delivery business model use classes of service appropriately, based on an understanding of business risks (for example, the cost of delay) to facilitate selection decisions and inspire **queuing discipline** policies for work items? Are you understanding customer expectations and how they cluster into similar groups? Are you probing for possible new classes of service to improve the flow of value to the customer?
- Is there capacity in the system to hedge risks from different sources of demand and different types of work? For example, can resources be diverted to priority tasks during high-demand periods?
- Are interdependent services aggregated and coordinated to increase **system liquidity** and enable **system leveling** in light of risks and variability?

Kanban Roles

Kanban is and remains the "start with what you do now" method, where initially no one receives new roles, responsibilities, or job titles. So there are no required roles in Kanban and the method does not create new positions in the organization. However, two roles have emerged from common practice in the field and are now defined in the method itself. It is the *purpose* of the roles that is important, rather than assigning someone a job title, so it may be helpful to think of the roles as "hats" people wear in carrying out these functions:

- The *Service Request Manager* is responsible for understanding the needs and expectations of customers, and for facilitating selecting and ordering work items at the Replenishment Meeting. Alternative names for the role are Product Manager, Product Owner, and Service Manager.
- The *Service Delivery Manager* is responsible for the flow of work in delivering selected items to customers and for facilitating the Kanban Meeting and Delivery Planning. Alternative names for this role are Flow Manager, Delivery Manager, or even Flow Master.

Forecasting and Metrics

Forecasting accurately when services will be delivered to customers has long been a difficult management problem. Traditionally, projects have used "effort-plus-risk estimating" to forecast completion dates. Kanban systems enable an alternative (some would say more reliable) method—**probabilistic forecasting**.

Traditional effort-plus-risk approaches break down a large piece of work (like a project) into very small items and then sum the effort estimates for these items. Then either an acceptable date or the team size is agreed upon, which leaves the other variable to be determined by ensuring that the lead time multiplied by the team size is greater than the estimated effort by a sufficiently large factor to account for risks and profit. Often this involves a "risk factor" of between 2 and 10. This method has often proven spectacularly unsuccessful on all sizes of projects, but particularly on large and critical ones. Surprisingly, it still is the dominant method of forecasting.

Kanban systems, once established, provide the opportunity to base forecasting on the observed flow of value (encapsulated in much smaller work items than typical projects) delivered through established teams. Probabilistic forecasting works by using a simple model of the existing teams (or similarly structured new ones), where some data has already been gathered on item size variability, lead times, and delivery rates. If there is no data available from similar teams, range estimates can be used until actual data starts flowing. Using a **Monte Carlo method,** which runs scenarios multiple times, the percentage likelihood of a range of completion dates can be generated. Providing this to planners encourages a better approach to balancing

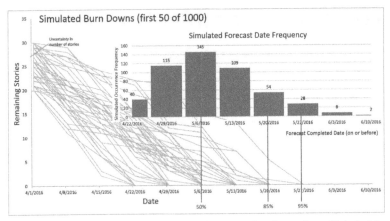

Figure 11 Probabilistic Forecast showing the uncertainty in number of "stories" to complete and the Delivery Rate. Completion Dates with 50%, 85%, and 95% probabilities are marked.

cost and risk with schedules and commitments. Figure 11 shows the output from a Monte Carlo model run, showing a selection of the many randomized simulations carried out, and the resulting Forecast Date distribution, which is the basis of the probabilistic forecast.

Designing appropriate service level agreements with customers is also enabled by collecting actual data from kanban systems and applying statistical analysis and probabilistic forecasting.

Flow systems can provide a wide range of flow metrics that are important to the managers of these systems, particularly for producing reliable forecasts.[17] The minimum starting point is to collect data on Lead Time, Delivery Rate, WiP, and cost (usually primarily the effort in person-days consumed by the service).

Probabilistic forecasting works best when actual historical data on the performance of services is available (second best is a well considered range estimate). Significant analysis of many types of systems is now becoming available, which enables services to predict the shape of lead time or delivery rate distributions.[18]

The metrics captured in the graphs in Figures 12, 13 and 14 were generated simply from the dates when items entered the states of "Committed," "Acceptance," and "Delivered." Some cost data, in terms of either financial costs or person-days, also should be captured.

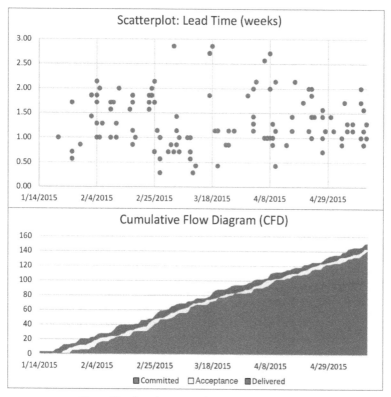

Figure 12 Complementary charts of the same flow data

Top: Scatterplot of Lead Times for items on their delivery dates

Bottom: Cumulative Flow Diagram showing the cumulative number of items Committed, in Acceptance, and Delivered by date

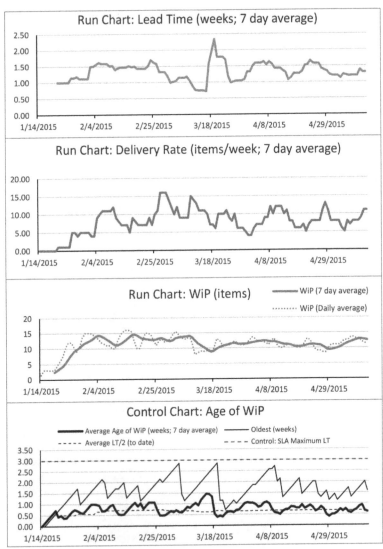

Figure 13 Run or control charts of LT, DR, WiP, and Age of WiP

There are several important types of graphs for displaying flow systems data, including:

- **Scatterplots** of Lead Times (see Figure 12)

- **Cumulative Flow Diagrams** (CFDs), which show the cumulative number of arrivals and departures in a process or in parts of a process (see Figure 12)
- **Run Charts** of average Lead Times, Delivery Rates, WiP, and **Age of WiP** (see Figure 13)
- **Control Charts** of Lead Times or Age of WiP may also be used. Control charts may be run charts or scatterplots with the addition of control ranges, which may be used to trigger action that keeps items in the desired range. Control charts are more common in manufacturing than in Kanban because of the higher natural and expected variation in knowledge work (see Figure 13).
- **Distribution Histograms** of Lead Times and Delivery Rates (see example in Figure 14)

The run charts in Figure 13 show the variation in the 7-day rolling averages for these metrics over the same period. The Age of WiP chart additionally shows the age of the "oldest" item in progress. It

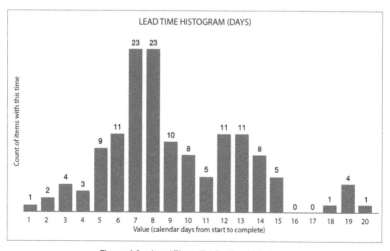

Figure 14   Lead Time distribution histogram

is a control chart due to the addition of control lines, which trigger analysis or intervention.

Distribution data is needed for effective probabilistic forecasting. Figure 14 shows an example of a Lead Time distribution histogram. Relying on a single value (like an average) for forecasting or making decisions is problematic because it hides patterns of different types of data and context. Some ranges of values will occur more often than others, and often in a Kanban process there are multiple peaks (very common values) and troughs (rarer values). The peaks commonly represent different types of work, different priority of work, or class of service promises. To improve predictability of a system delivery to customer, it is important to consider this distribution of values so that the right range is chosen for the work type or class of service you are analyzing.

Expanding the Application of Kanban

How do you scale Kanban? The answer is simple: by applying Kanban in a context of greater scale.

Once kanban systems are established for one or more services, consider three dimensions in which they can grow within your organization.

Width-wise growth   Encompass a wider scope of the work items' lifecycle by expanding the end-to-end workflow both up- and down-stream (see Figure 15). For example, if the original service models only the development team's process, explore what happens before the items enter development and after they exit as "done." A wider scope for the process reveals potentially more areas for effectively improving the service to customers.

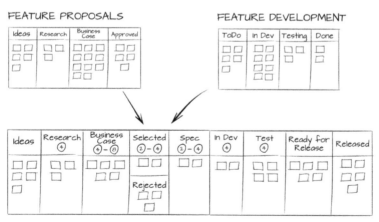

Figure 15   Width-wise growth example. This board also shows the use of minimum and maximum WiP limits.

Height-wise growth   Consider the hierarchy of items that make up deliveries, each level potentially having differing flow characteristics. For example, a "user story" is a small part of the functionality of a software product "feature," which is part of a software release. Kanban may be used at each of these levels—with differing workflows and policies at each level. This dimension uses the "scale-free" nature of Kanban: the same principles and general practices apply whatever the size of the work item, even though the nature of work at the different scales entails very different systems and policies (Figure 16).

Four specific levels are often identified:

1. *Personal*   For example, the use of **Personal Kanban**[19] for an individual or small team to foster efficient and effective working

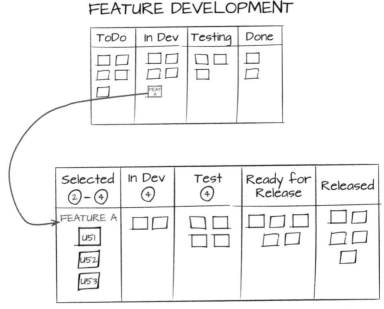

Figure 16   Height-wise growth example

2. *Team*   Understanding the team's work as a "service" and applying Kanban practices to create a predictable flow of value

3. *Product or Service Delivery*   Product management requires the effective coordination of options for enhancements and the flow of customer-valued changes for competitive advantage. The work items should be considerably larger than those at the team level, and generally recognizable by a customer or user of a product, but much smaller than typical projects.

4. *Portfolio*   At this level, Kanban supports investment-level decisions concerning which new and existing projects need greater or less investment to deliver change. Portfolio management is not a variant of project management with bigger projects, but a completely different discipline, more aligned with managing financial portfolios. Balancing risk in the portfolio by considering different time horizons for return on investment, and multiple options to address different outcomes and market changes, contribute to building more resilient, antifragile[20] organizations.

Depth-wise growth   A deep implementation of Kanban needs not only greater depth of understanding, but depth of penetration through the full set of services required by the organization to deliver value. Depth-wise growth connects multiple services at the same level through the feedback loops (cadences) that balance the capacity across the services. Figure 17 shows how items blocked in one service may be dependent on other specialist services. A service might provide a specific function (legal, IT, HR, or accounting services, for example) or be aligned around the delivery of work that requires widely differing skill sets within them (new product development or film and television services, for example). The challenge in the extended Kanban ecosystem is to achieve balance and flow across all of the interdependent services.

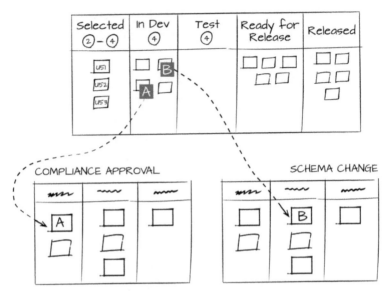

Figure 17   Depth-wise growth example

A note of caution: Kanban's values, principles, and practices are defined without regard to scale. However, examples, explanations, and advice may well be tailored to specific assumptions concerning scale and context. The complexity is always greater at larger scale, so particular care must be taken not to carry over assumptions from one scale to a larger one or, indeed, between differing contexts of flow systems with very different characteristics.

An important recent development in the evolution of Kanban and its application across large organizations is **Enterprise Services Planning (ESP)**.[21] This has a management training syllabus that provides managers with the knowledge and confidence to apply Kanban in networks of potentially hundreds of interdependent services. While ESP is outside the scope of this book, it does use the definition of Kanban described here. This is foundational material that is essential to understand in the context of ESP.

Learning More about Kanban

This book's goal is to provide the *essence* of the method in a compact and accessible form, and to point the way forward for students of the method to discover more and to participate in its ongoing evolution. What follows is a list of publications that extend the current definition of the method, including rationale, examples, and case studies.

Although this book summarizes the principal elements of Kanban, these concepts are defined and explained in more depth in the original "Blue Book," *Kanban: Successful Evolutionary Change for Your Technology Business* (Anderson, 2010). This is the seminal publication on the Kanban Method, and it provides essential background, examples, and rationale for its practices.

More recent texts on the method, such as *Kanban From the Inside* (Burrows, 2014) and *Kanban Change Leadership* (Leopold, 2015), give more detail. *Kanban From the Inside* defines, amplifies, and explains the values of Kanban and how its principles and practices flow from them. It also usefully tracks influences and sources for many of Kanban's practices, and discusses its relation to other approaches such as Lean, Theory of Constraints, and Agile. *Kanban Change Leadership* explains how to establish a culture of continuous improvement in Kanban implementations, and it has useful summaries of both the practices of the method and how to apply them in change initiatives. Several case studies on Kanban implementations are available as downloadable papers from the Lean Kanban University (LKU) web site (Dzhambazova, 2015). Together, these materials provide the foundational knowledge base for those wishing to understand the method.

In addition to these sources, there are many books describing current Kanban practice and its relationship to other methods. *Kanban in Action* (Hammarberg, 2014) provides an accessible way to start using many of the Kanban's practices, particularly visualizing, limiting work in progress, and managing flow. Another practical Kanban book is *Real-World Kanban* (Skarin, 2015), which explains the practices in the context of a number of real-world examples. We've already mentioned *Personal Kanban* (Benson, 2011), which is a great way to get a small team started with Kanban, or even just to organize your home life. The lessons it provides have wider application and even help when you're scaling up to large or multiple services. Along similar lines is Jim Benson's *Why Limit WIP: We Are Drowning in Work* (Benson, 2015).

To really understand Kanban, it is also worth looking not only to current and future authors on the method, but to those who laid the foundations for the method with the Toyota Production System and Lean Manufacturing,[22] Systems Thinking,[23] and the Theory of Constraints.[24] Not everything in these methods found their way into the Kanban Method, but the insights from these authors continue to inspire and influence Kanban practitioners today.

Remember that this book is a compact guide—it is not a tutorial on how to implement Kanban. Please don't use it as an excuse to apply literal interpretations blindly and make avoidable mistakes! Kanban has principles and general practices, but these must be applied in context, where different details will emerge as we pursue the common agendas of sustainability, service-orientation, and survivability. As a result, the journey is an adventure into unknown territory rather than a march over familiar ground. The journey may never be complete, but every step can be worthwhile.

Glossary

Many of the definitions in this Glossary draw significantly, in some cases word for word, from the Kanban Glossary published in Kanban from the Inside *(Burrows, 2014) and on the Lean Kanban University web site (LKU, 2015). They are used here with permission.*

Abort   To **discard** a work item after the **commitment point**.
Related terms: **commitment point, discard**

Activity   In the context of a **workflow,** identified activities are performed on **work items** that are in appropriate states; activities often take work items from one **state** to another. Activities and their corresponding states typically map to the columns on a **kanban board.**

Age of WiP   The amount of time that a **work item** currently in progress has been in progress. The term may also apply to the average of all items in progress.
Measured in: units of time[25]
Related term: **work in progress (WiP)**

Agendas   In the context of **Kanban,** an agenda (or agenda for change) is a compelling call to action based on organizational need. Three agendas of Kanban are sustainability, customer delivery, and survivability.

Blocker   A **work item** is said to be blocked when there is some abnormal condition preventing it from progressing. This condition, or the "proximate cause," may be referred to as the **blocker** (often requiring work or resources from outside the team or **service**). Blockers may be visualized on the **kanban board** with an indicator attached to the work item, for example, with a pink sticker.

Blocker clustering   A risk analysis technique that uses records of issues that have blocked work items, grouping them by common cause.

Cadence   A review or meeting providing feedback from one or more **services**. Cadence also refers to the time period between reviews.

Card   A visual representation of a **work item**.
Alternative: ticket or **kanban (2)**.

Classes of service   Categories of **work items** that may warrant different **policies** for selection and processing based on different customer expectations, relative value, risk, or **cost of delay**. Four archetypes of class of service are widely recognized: "standard" (the baseline class), "fixed date" (date-driven—the point at which there is a rapid or steep change in **CoD**), "expedite" (very high **urgency**), and "intangible" (low current **urgency** but likely to change significantly at an indeterminate point in the future).

Commitment point   The point in a **kanban system** at which the commitment is made to deliver a **work item**. Before this point, work done supports the decision whether or not to deliver the item. After this point, it has been confirmed that the customer wants and will take delivery of the item, and that the **service** will deliver it.
Related terms: **abort, delivery point**

Control chart   A chart, usually a **run chart** or **scatterplot**, showing control ranges outside of which a process may be considered "out of control" in some specific sense. It may be used to trigger root cause or other analysis of **Lead Time** outliers. Control charts have limited use in **Kanban** because of the greater natural and expected variation in **knowledge work** compared to manufacturing.
Related terms: **run chart, scatterplot**

Cost of Delay (CoD)   The rate at which the value of a product, initiative or **work item** decays when its delivery is delayed; that is, the **Delay Cost** per unit of time. Cost of Delay may be used to inform time-related decisions, including the ordering of items during **replenishment** (see for example **WSJF**). The plot of CoD against delay period is referred to as the **Urgency** Profile.

Measured in: value per units of time (e.g., dollars per week)

Alternative term: **Urgency**, Real Urgency, Delay Cost Gradient

Related terms: **Delay Cost, WSJF**

Cumulative Flow Diagram (CFD)   A chart showing the cumulative number of arrivals and departures from a process, or parts of a process, over a time period.

Related terms: **control chart, run chart, scatterplot**

Customer Lead Time   The time a customer waits for a **work item**. Typically, this is measured from the request for a **service** to the receipt of the service.

Measured in: units of time

Related terms: **Lead Time, System Lead Time, Time in Process**

Cycle Time (CT1, CT2)   The time it takes for a "cycle." This is an ambiguous term that should not be used in **Kanban** without qualification or further definition. It may be applied to the time between two items emerging from a process[26] (**CT1**)—for example, the period between releases of new builds of software—or to the time between starting and completing an item[27] (**CT2**)—for example, the time it takes to develop a product feature. **CT1** is sometimes compared with a target or expected value, known as the **Takt Time**, in order to coordinate processing in different **activities**.

Measured in: units of time

Alternatives: For **CT1**, use its reciprocal—**Delivery Rate** or **Throughput**; for CT2, use **Lead Time** or **Time in Process**.

Deferred commitment   Separating the request for work from the commitment to do work, so that the system operates as a **pull system**.

Delay Cost   The difference between the benefit (e.g., **net present value** or lifetime profits) that would be available from a product, initiative, or **work item** if it were completed without delay, and the benefit if it were delayed by a period of time. The first derivative or gradient of this term (the rate at which the Delay Cost changes) is referred to as the **Urgency** or **Cost of Delay**. The plot of Delay Cost against delay period is referred to as the Delay Cost Profile.

Measured in: consistent units of value (e.g., monetary currency)
Related terms: **Cost of Delay, classes of service, WSJF**

Delivery point   The point at which an item is considered to be delivered or complete.

Related term: **commitment point**

Delivery Rate (DR)   The number of **work items** emerging complete from the **system** per unit of time.

Measured in: ratio of work items per unit of time
Alternative: Completion Rate
Related term: **Throughput**

Discard   To stop work on an item and remove it from the part of the process under consideration. The term is not specific about when in the process the item is discarded; however, in a **kanban system** it applies particularly to items discarded prior to the **commitment point**, since after this point the term **abort** is applicable.

Related terms: abort, commitment point

Discovery Kanban   The application of **Kanban** to finding the most advantageous work to do in the context of innovation and change.[28]

Alternative: Upstream Kanban

Distribution histogram   A graph showing the number of occurrences of a given value (for example, of **Lead Time**) in a dataset. The distribution of a metric's values, not just its average, is needed for effective **probabilistic forecasting**.

Enterprise Services Planning (ESP)   An approach to managing large networks of **services**, applying **Kanban** at each level of management and within each service.

Fitness landscape   A term borrowed from evolutionary biology to visualize, as a multi-dimensional landscape, the fitness of an entity with different traits to the prevailing environment.[29]

Flow Efficiency   The ratio of the time spent working on an item (**Touch Time**) to the total **Time in Process**.
Measured in: percentage
Related term: **Resource Efficiency**

Flow system   A **system** characterized by the entry and departure of **work items**. It is a way of viewing **knowledge work** by the flow of items from the request or idea through to its delivered value.
Related term: **kanban system**

Kanban (1)   A method for defining, managing, and improving **services** that deliver **knowledge work**.
Alternative: **The Kanban Method**

Kanban (2)   A kanban is a signal, usually a visual signal, used in **kanban systems** to indicate demand or available capacity, and to limit **WiP**.

Kanban board   A board with a visual display of the **cards** in a **kanban system**. Typically, kanban boards are arranged in vertical columns with (optionally) horizontal **swimlanes**; additional dimensions may be represented by color or other card attributes. Cards move rightward from column to column as the **work items** they represent progress through the system. **WiP limits** and other **policies** may also be represented visually on the board.

Kanban Meeting The meeting in front of the **kanban board** that is both a core social aspect of the method and the most fundamental feedback mechanism, or **cadence**. It typically occurs daily, and its focus is more on the flow of the work than on the **activities** of **service** participants.

Kanban system A **flow system** with defined **commitment** and **delivery points**, and with **work in progress limits**.
Related terms: **pull system, kanban (2), protokanban**

Knowledge work Work that is done primarily by using and developing knowledge; work performed by knowledge workers.
Related term: **Kanban (1)**

Lead Time (LT) The elapsed time it takes for a **work item** to move from the **commitment point** to the **delivery point**. Informally, or if qualified, it may refer to the time it takes to move through a different part of the process; see, for example, **Customer Lead Time**.
Measured in: units of time
Alternative: **System Lead Time**
Related terms: **Time in Process (TiP), Customer Lead Time**

Little's Law A simple relationship between the attributes of queues and **flow systems**. Originally formulated as a relationship between arrival rate, queue length, and wait time,[5] for **kanban systems** it may be expressed as:

$$\overline{Delivery\ Rate} = \frac{\overline{WiP}}{\overline{Lead\ Time}} \quad \text{or as} \quad \overline{Throughput} = \frac{\overline{WiP}}{\overline{TiP}}$$

where the overline indicates the arithmetic mean over a given period. To apply exactly, the system must be statistically *stationary*[30] (non-trending), or be between two points of zero **WiP**, and items must not be "lost" from the system (i.e., from **discards** or **aborts**).

Monte Carlo methods   A broad class of computational algorithms that rely on repeated random sampling to obtain numerical results.[31] *Related term*: **probabilistic forecasting**

Net Present Value (NPV)   The present value of future cash flows (such as the benefits of a delivered **work item** or project) that takes into account the opportunity cost of capital and the risk that anticipated benefits may not occur.

Options   Options represent the right—though not the obligation—to carry out an action or use a resource. Like financial options, all options have value and an expiration condition at the point their value reduces to zero. They are important in **Kanban** since a work item before the **commitment point** represents an option to deliver the item or not.
Alternative: **Real options**

Personal Kanban   The application of **Kanban** to the workload of an individual or small team. In the book of the same name,[18] the authors highlight two of the six **Kanban** practices as particularly relevant at this scale: *Visualize* and *Limit Work in Progress*.

Probabilistic forecasting   An approach to forecasting outcomes from a **flow system** that uses data of previous **Delivery Rates** and **Lead Times** combined with a **Monte Carlo** or similar method.

Policy   An explicit description of expected behavior or a process constraint. Policies commonly associated with **kanban systems** include column-level "definitions of ready." **WiP limits** are also classified as policies.

Related term: **queueing discipline**

Protokanban   A **flow system** or process where the **Kanban Method** is being applied, but which does not yet show characteristics of a mature system; for example, where **work in progress** is not controlled between the **commitment** and **delivery points**.

Related terms: **kanban system, WiP**

Pull system   A system for scheduling and delivering work only when both demand exists and delivery capacity is available. No work item is started without both a request for the item and capacity within the **system** to deliver it. A **kanban system** is an example of a pull system that uses **WiP Limits** to represent the available capacity and to signal the need to pull items when capacity is available.

Related terms: **kanban system, WiP, WiP Limit**

Queue   A place in a **workflow** (typically represented by a column on a **kanban board**) in which **work items** are held ahead of some later **activity**.

Queuing discipline   The set of policies that govern the selection of **work items**. First in first out (FIFO) and **Weighted Shortest Job First (WSJF)** are two examples.

Replenishment   The act of populating the input **queue** for a **service**.

Related term: Replenishment Meeting

Resource Efficiency   The ratio of the amount of time a resource (for example, a person!) is actively working on a work item to that resource's total available time. This measure is generally not used in

Kanban, except possibly to check that it is not too high, since very high Resource Efficiency blocks flow and lengthens **Lead Time**.

Measured in: percentage

Related term: **Flow Efficiency**

Run chart   A chart that shows an observed metric in a time sequence. It is commonly used to visualize the running average of **Lead Times** or **Delivery Rates**.

Alternative: run-sequence plot

Related term: **control chart**

Scatterplot   A chart that shows individual data points from a data-set plotted on an X-Y grid; commonly used to see the individual **Lead Times** of **work items** plotted against their delivery dates.

Related terms: **Cumulative Flow Diagram, run chart**

Scrumban   The application of **Kanban** in the context of an existing implementation of Scrum. Colloquially, it is Kanban when the "what you do now" is Scrum.[32]

Service   One or more people collaborating to produce (usually intangible) work products for a customer who requests the work and who accepts or acknowledges delivery of the completed work. The term may also apply to the work product that the service delivers.

Related term: **knowledge work**

State   The overall condition of a **work item** that determines where it should be in the system and what **activity** or activities could legitimately be applied to it.

Related terms: **activity, workflow**

STATIK   An acronym for the *Systems Thinking Approach to Implementing Kanban*, a recommended approach to introducing **Kanban** in a new context.

Swimlane   a horizontal lane on a **kanban board** crossing two or more columns along which **cards** flow. Swimlanes organize cards into categories, such as the type of the **work item**, the customer requiring the work, or its **class of service**.

System   A complex and dynamic construct or community of parts through which people, materials, information, and energy flows, changing and being changed. The behavior of both the whole and the parts of the system is relevant, but it is the holistic nature of the system that is of paramount concern in "systems thinking." In the context of this book, we are concerned primarily with social and organizational systems.

System Lead Time   See **Lead Time**.

System leveling   Moving resources or people among types of work to maintain the highest level of value flowing to customers.

System liquidity   The ability of a **system** to respond to new and varied requests for work. It is dependent on the volume of **work items** that may be processed concurrently and the staff's flexibility to handle different types of work.

Takt Time   The projected customer demand expressed as the average unit production time (i.e., the average time between the completion of **work items**) that would be needed to meet this demand. It may be used to synchronize various sub-processes within a **system** being designed so as to meet demand without over or under production.
Measured in: units of time
Related terms: **Cycle Time (CT1)**, **Delivery Rate**

Throughput   The number of **work items** exiting a **system** or sub-system per unit of time, whether completed or **discarded**.
Measured in: work items per unit of time (e.g., items per working day)
Alternatives: Throughput Rate, Departure Rate, Processing Rate
Related term: **Delivery Rate**

Time in Process (TiP)   The total time that a **work item** remains in a **state** under consideration. More specific terms may be derived by replacing "Process" with a particular part of the process of interest, for example, *Time in Development, Time in Test,* or *Time in Queue.* Depending on the state of interest, the time may not be contiguous; TiP is the sum of all of the periods in that state.[33]

Measured in: units of time

Alternatives: **Lead Time** (when referring to the time in process from the **commitment** to **delivery point**), Time in System

Related terms: **Cycle Time (CT2), Lead Time**

Touch Time   The sum of all the times during which a **work item** is actively being worked on (excluding wait times; e.g., being held in stock or in queues).

Measured in: units of time

Related terms: **TiP, Lead Time, Flow Efficiency**

Unbounded queue   A **queue** or stage in a process that does not have a **WiP limit.** Such a stage may be shown as a column on a **kanban board** without a WiP limit or with the symbol ∞ to indicate that it is unconstrained.

Alternative: Infinite queue

Urgency   See **Cost of Delay.** Urgency is the preferred term in contexts where confusion may arise between **Cost of Delay** and **Delay Cost.**

Values   In the context of **Kanban,** values refer to properties and behaviors that are widely agreed to be desirable, provide some sense of direction (because "more is better," generally speaking), and serve to suggest, organize, or represent helpful practices and artifacts. The nine values of Kanban (transparency, balance, collaboration, customer focus, flow, leadership, understanding, agreement, and respect) are abstracted from the method's practices and principles.

Other schools of thought and different organizational cultures will emphasize different values; values can be useful, therefore, for the purposes of comparison and selection.

Related term: **agendas**

Weighted Shortest Job First (WSJF)   A **queuing discipline** that seeks to minimize **cost of delay** by giving precedence to **work items** that have the largest economic impact in proportion to the remaining time needed to implement them.[34]

Workflow   The sequencing of **activities** and/or **work item states** that results in products or **services** being delivered. Workflows tend to cut across considerations of functional structure, though not always optimally.

Work item   A deliverable or a component thereof that will be worked on by the **service** (a new product feature, for example).

Related terms: **card, workflow**

Work in Progress (WiP)   The **work items** that have entered the **system** or **state** under consideration, but that have not yet been either completed or **discarded**.

Measured in: count of work items

Related terms: **Throughput, TiP, Delivery Rate, Lead Time**

Work in Progress Limit (WiP Limit)   A **policy** that constrains the amount of **WiP** allowed in a given part of the **system**. WiP-limited systems are **pull systems**. Maximum limits prevent starting new work when there is insufficient downstream capacity to complete the work. Minimum limits trigger **replenishment** when there is downstream capacity.

Measured in: count of **work items**

Notes

Notes from all chapters and the Glossary.

1. A **kanban** is a general term for a physical or virtual entity that limits WiP. The more common term in the Kanban Method is simply a "WiP Limit."

2. The values of Kanban were identified by Mike Burrows in his book *Kanban From The Inside* (Burrows, 2014) following workshops with Kanban coaches and projects. The values relate closely to the agendas, principles, and general practices of Kanban.

3. Or "Upstream Kanban." See (Steyaert, 2014) for more information about Discovery Kanban.

4. Or that is between two points of zero WiP.

5. The original proof of Little's Law appeared in *Operations Research* in 1961 (Little, 1961). Interesting insights into both the proof and subsequent applications of the law appeared in the 50th anniversary of that paper (Little, 2011).

6. (Maccherone, 2012). Note that some authors use Cycle Time (CT2) for this quantity. See the Glossary for the definitions of CT1 and CT2, and an explanation of why Cycle Time is not a recommended term in the Kanban Method. Also see note 33.

7. A further distinction may be drawn between Throughput and Delivery Rate even if the point at which it is measured is identical. Throughput includes all items that depart from the system under consideration, whether they were delivered, aborted, or discarded.

8. This is from one of the case studies available on the LKU web site (Dzhambazova, 2015).

9. Evidence for the positive impact of limiting WiP on quality and other customer outcomes comes from, among other sources, *The Impact of Agile, Quantified* (Maccherone, 2015). This showed strong correlation between teams that limited WiP and improved defect rates. Larry Maccherone's work examining Agile practices in over 10,000 teams was presented at the Lean Kanban conferences in Chicago and London in 2014 (Maccherone, 2014).

10. The concept that keeping staff busy might be an ineffective way of managing will be so counterintuitive to many managers that further justification is probably needed.

    There are several aspects to excessive WiP that are relevant to effectiveness, among them multi-tasking, context switching, focus, and long lead times. Recent research on the brain has shown that one of the most expensive things your brain does (in terms of energy consumption) is changing tasks (Levitin, 2015). Doing it constantly is draining and ineffective. Focusing on one task, for periods of around 90 minutes at a time, enables your brain to get into the state known as *flow*. That's when your most effective work gets done, and amazingly, it makes you feel good while tiring you out less. Periods of flow are not your most creative periods, however. Focus is your brain's mode when you "get things done," but in your brain's default mode, your mind flits between ideas. This is when you make connections between things and where creativity springs from. It is also where learning and long-term memories are created. To be effective, you need time at work to be in both these modes; constant pressure with multiple unfinished tasks is damaging to both modes and results in poorer outcomes.

    For more on this topic, see (Benson, 2014).

11. For another, or complementary, approach to item ordering, see note 34 below on **WSJF**.

12. The term "Lean flow paradigm" was highlighted by Rodrigo Yoshima (2013) in his LKNA presentation "Management and Change—Avoiding the Rocks."

13. For a more detailed analysis of how processes and technologies have evolved, and how this evolution is influenced by and contributes to complex economies, see *The Origin of Wealth* (Beinhocker, 2007).

14. A tweetable version of "How to adopt Kanban" emerged in 2013—*See flow; Start here; With visible work and policies, make validated improvements.* (Carmichael, 2013)

15. Protokanban was a term first coined by the academic Richard Turner, Distinguished Service Professor at the Stevens Institute of Technology. Richard and David Anderson were discussing, over a period of several days, Garcia and Turner's *CMMI Survival Guide* (2006) and its application to Kanban. The term protokanban came from the observation that these incomplete kanban systems are often evolutionary forerunners of a genuine, WiP-limited pull system using Kanban.

16. See, for example, (Meadows, 2009). Systems Thinking is foundational to the Kanban Method and influences many aspects of its definition and application.

17. See, for example, *Actionable Agile Metrics for Predictability: An Introduction* (Vacanti, 2015).

18. In recent years, the major contribution to the practical application of probabilistic forecasting for flow systems in knowledge work has come from Troy Magennis (2011). As well as sharing several very useful spreadsheets and other software for the practical application of probabilistic forecasting (Magennis, 2016), he has contributed important insights into variation in knowledge work.

His empirical examination of a large number of datasets from Agile and non-Agile development projects, and his theoretical analysis of how normally distributed blockers cause "fat tails" in the distribution, has shown that Lead Times in such projects approximate to Weibull distributions (Weibull, 1951). Weibull distributions cover a wide range of typical distributions (including Exponential and Raleigh). They are characterized by two parameters, the shape parameter (controlling where the highest peak falls, designated k below) and the scale parameter (controlling how wide the tail extends, designated λ below). Troy compared dataset fits for different types of projects showing the Raleigh distribution of Waterfall projects ($k = 2$), was left-shifted in the case of Agile projects (to $k = 1.5$), with mode and median proportionately lower compared to the mean, but with "fatter tails" (Magennis, 2015).

This information is useful for projects with much smaller amounts of data available to them, since they can project what data they have onto these theoretical models, improving progressively as more data becomes available.

19. *Personal Kanban* (Benson, 2011).

20. This adjective was coined by Nassim Nicholas Taleb in *Antifragile: Things That Gain from Disorder* (2013). He discusses how hierarchies can gain antifragility by allowing fragility within them, and how natural antifragility can be irresponsibly eroded if higher structures in the hierarchies (like governments and portfolio managers) absorb the fragility of structures within them (like banks and products). By maintaining multiple products within a portfolio that target different sectors and timescales, the organization has the opportunity to gain from disruptive change rather than being threatened by it.

21. Training in Enterprise Service Planning is available from Lean Kanban Services (Anderson, 2015a). Overviews of the approach may be viewed online, for example (Anderson, 2015b).

22. See, for example, (Liker, 2004) and (Womack, 2003).

23. Systems thinkers abound in the inspiring figures who have influenced Kanban. *Thinking in Systems* (Meadows, 2009) is hard to beat as an introduction to this subject, but the writings of Drucker, Deming, Senge, Weinberg, and many others should also be mentioned. *The Landmarks of Tomorrow* (Drucker, 1959) is the first work to use the phrase "knowledge worker." Of the many works that could be referenced by the other authors, *The New Economics* (Deming, 2000) and *The Essential Deming* (Deming, 2012) are included, as both have useful chapters on systems, among the many other insightful observations on their application in management.

24. See, for example, *The Goal: A Process of Ongoing Improvement* (Goldratt, 1989).

25. "Units of time" is used throughout the glossary. Clearly, years, weeks, days, hours, and even seconds might all be used. A slight complication arises over whether to include or exclude non-working time, such as weekends and company holidays. When specifying the units, this should be made clear, for example, by stating calendar days or working days. This applies even when using units like weeks, where weekends might appear not to matter. It does affect how, for example, an Average Lead Time of 0.5 weeks is interpreted.

26. *Lean Lexicon* (Shook, 2014).

27. *Factory Physics* (Hopp, 2005).

28. *Discovery Kanban* (Steyaert, 2014).

29. *Fitness Landscape* (Wikipedia, 2015a).

30. *Stationary* (Wikipedia, 2015c).

31. *Monte Carlo Methods* (Wikipedia, 2015b).

32. Many people ask about how Kanban fits with Scrum (Schwaber, 2013), the mostly widely used method in the Agile community at the team level. Henrik Kniberg and Mattias Skarin addressed the practicalities of this in their book *Kanban and Scrum: Making The Most of Both* (2010). The first author to use the term "Scrumban" in a book was Corey Ladas, in *Scrumban* (2009), where he looked at how applying Kanban, when you are currently using Scrum, might change standard practices of that method. This has been picked up and expanded more recently in Ajay Reddy's *The Scrumban [R]Evolution* (Reddy, 2016), which discusses many of the themes introduced in *Essential Kanban Condensed*.

33. Time in Process (TiP) as a term was introduced in (Maccherone, 2012). There are several advantages in using TiP over Cycle Time, not least that it does not suffer the same ambiguity through use by different authors in contradictory ways. However, care must be used when applying TiP in Little's Law to ensure that if items are allowed to move back in the workflow, arrivals and departures in the state are not double-counted. Backflows of work items are discouraged in Kanban, as progress is more clearly understandable if, when rework is required, the item is shown as blocked at the point it had reached in the process and, if necessary, a separate item is created to cover the rework task. If items need to be moved back to a place in the workflow that is before the commitment point, (unless this is just correcting an error) this should be considered, for flow metrics purposes, as equivalent to aborting the item and restarting with a new item at that point.

34. **Weighted Shortest Job First (WSJF)** was proposed by Don Reinertsen (2009) as a mechanism for ordering and selecting potential new product features. It seeks to maximize the business value that is delivered by a fixed capability resource, such as the product development team.

Consider a set of features to be put in order of development. The features have an estimated value, if completed without delay, of V (the **net current value** of all cash flows positive and negative during its completion and exploitation); an estimated development delay, D, which may be equal to the Lead Time if the feature has not yet been started and the commitment to start can be made immediately; and importantly, a **Delay Cost** profile, which indicates the amount of value lost by a given delay. The amount lost per week at any point in time (the gradient of the profile) is referred to as the **urgency** (or Cost of Delay), U, of the feature. In a system where the WiP limit is 1 (so the team does only 1 feature at a time), and assuming the urgency is a constant, the estimated value realized by 2 features—first feature 1, then feature 2—may be expressed as the sum of their values minus the cost of delay for each feature, thus:

$$V_1 + V_2 - U_1 D_1 - U_2(D_1 + D_2)$$

How, then, can we know whether it is more advantageous in realized value to do feature 1 or feature 2 first? Simply by subtracting the value above from the equivalent value with feature 2 completed first. This difference is:

$$\left(\frac{U_1}{D_1} - \frac{U_2}{D_2}\right) D_1 D_2$$

This provides us with the basic principle of WSJF, which is that items should be ordered by selecting the item with maximum urgency (or CoD) divided by its time to completion (if completed without delay). This favors shorter, more urgent jobs.

If urgency is not constant over the prioritization period—for example, if it is a "fixed date" item—the simple formula is not applicable, although the principle of picking the item that results in the least cost of delay still applies (see discussion of cost of delay on page page 21).

Often, the process of estimating CoD for items—particularly intangible items such as risk reduction work, exploration and learning, creation of options, and so on—is difficult and time consuming. In these cases, knowing the Delay Cost archetype (see discussion of classes of service on page page 21) is often sufficient to guide prioritization and queuing discipline decisions. For further discussion of the use of CoD in Kanban see (Carmichael, 2016).

References

Anderson (2005)
> David J. Anderson and Dragos Dumitriu. "From Worst to Best in 9 Months: Implementing a Drum-Buffer-Rope Solution at Microsoft's IT Department." *TOC ICO World Conference*, November 2005, USA: Microsoft Corporation.

Anderson (2010)
> David J. Anderson. *Kanban: Successful Evolutionary Change for Your Technology Business*. Sequim, WA: Blue Hole Press.

Anderson (2015a)
> David J. Anderson. "Introducing Enterprise Services Planning." *Lean Kanban Services*. http://services. leankanban.com/introducing-enterprise-services-planning (accessed March 18, 2016).

Anderson (2015b)
> David J. Anderson. "Kanban Enterprise Services Planning: Scaling the Benefits of Kanban." *London Limited WIP Society*, October 2015. http://www.slideshare.net/agilemanager/ enterprise-services-planning-scaling-the-benefits-of-kanban-54207714 (accessed November 2, 2015).

Beinhocker (2007)
> Eric D. Beinhocker. *The Origin of Wealth: Evolution, Complexity, and the Radical Remaking of Economics*. London: Random House Business Books.

Benson (2011)

> Jim Benson and Tonianne DeMaria Barry. *Personal Kanban: Mapping Work, Navigating Life.* Seattle, WA: Modus Cooperandi.

Benson (2014)

> Jim Benson. *Why Limit WIP: We Are Drowning in Work.* Seattle, WA: Modus Cooperandi.

Burrows (2014)

> Mike Burrows. *Kanban from the Inside: Understand the Kanban Method, connect it to what you already know, introduce it with impact.* Sequim, WA: Blue Hole Press.

Carmichael (2013)

> Andy Carmichael. "Shortest Possible Guide to Adopting Kanban." *Improving Projects.* http://xprocess.blogspot. co.uk/2013/ 05/how-to-adopt-kanban.html (accessed December 11, 2015).

Carmichael (2016)

> Andy Carmichael. "Understanding Cost of Delay and Its Use in Kanban." *Improving projects.* http://xprocess. blogspot.co.uk/2016/04/understanding-cost-of-delay-and-its-use.html (accessed April 15, 2016).

Deming (2000)

> W. Edwards Deming. *The New Economics: For Industry, Government, Education*, 2nd ed. Cambridge, MA: MIT Press.

Deming (2012)

> W. Edwards Deming. *The Essential Deming: Leadership Principles from the Father of Total Quality Management*, eds. Joyce Orsini and Diana Deming Cahill. New York: McGraw-Hill Professional Publishing.

Drucker (1959)

Peter F. Drucker. *The Landmarks of Tomorrow.* New York: Harper & Row.

Dzhambazova (2015)

Irina Dzhambazova. "Kanban Case Study Series." *Lean Kanban University.* http://leankanban.com/case-studies/ (accessed March 1, 2016).

Garcia (2006)

Suzanne Garcia and Richard Turner. *CMMI Survival Guide: Just Enough Process Improvement.* Upper Saddle River, NJ: Addison-Wesley.

Goldratt (1989)

Eliyahu M. Goldratt and Jeff Cox. *The Goal: A Process of Ongoing Improvement.* New York: North River Press.

Hammarberg (2014)

Marcus Hammarberg and Joakim Sunden. *Kanban in Action.* Shelter Island, NY: Manning Publications.

Hopp (2005)

Wallace J. Hopp and Mark L. Spearman. *Factory Physics,* 3rd ed. Long Grove, IL: Waveland Press.

Kniberg (2010)

Henrik Kniberg and Mattias Skarin. *Kanban and Scrum - Making the Most of Both.* United States: C4Media Inc. for InfoQ.

Ladas (2009)

Corey Ladas. *Scrumban and Other Essays on Kanban Systems for Lean Software Development.* Seattle, WA: Modus Cooperandi.

LKU (2015)

    "Glossary of Terms." *Lean Kanban University*. http://edu. leankanban.com/kanban-glossary-terms (accessed January 7, 2016).

Leopold (2015)

    Klaus Leopold and Siegfried Kaltenecker. *Kanban Change Leadership: Creating a Culture of Continuous Improvement.* Hoboken, NJ: John Wiley & Sons, Inc.

Liker (2004)

    Jeffrey K. Liker. *The Toyota Way: Fourteen Management Principles from the World's Greatest Manufacturer.* New York: McGraw-Hill.

Little (1961)

    John D. C. Little. "A Proof for the Queuing Formula: $L = \Lambda W$." *Operations Research*, 9(3): 383–87.

Little (2011)

    John D. C. Little. "Little's Law as Viewed on Its 50th Anniversary." *Operations Research*, 59(3): 536–49.

Levitin (2015)

    Daniel J. Levitin. *The Organized Mind: Thinking Straight in the Age of Information Overload.* London: Penguin Random House.

Maccherone (2012)

    Larry Maccherone, "Introducing the Time in State InSITe Visualization," ed. Eric Willeke, in Lean Software & Systems Conference 2012 (Boston, MA: Lean Software and Systems Consortium), http://leanssc.org/ files/2012-LSSC-Proceedings.pdf (accessed May 27, 2015).

Maccherone (2014)

> Larry Maccherone. "The Impact of Lean and Agile Quantified: 2014." *Lean Kanban UK 2014*, London: InfoQ. http://www.infoq.com/presentations/agile-quantify (accessed February 11, 2016).

Maccherone (2015)

> Larry Maccherone. "The Impact of Agile, Quantified." *CA Technologies*. https://www.rallydev.com/resource/impact-agile-quantified-sdpi-whitepaper (accessed February 10, 2016).

Magennis (2011)

> Troy Magennis. *Forecasting and Simulating Software Development Projects*. Focused Objective. http://focusedobjective.com/training/books-and-publications/ (accessed December 11, 2015).

Magennis (2015)

> Troy Magennis, "The Economic Impact of Software Development Process Choice — Cycle-Time Analysis and Monte Carlo Simulation Results," 48th Hawaii International Conference on System Sciences January 2015, doi:10.1109/hicss.2015.599.

Magennis (2016)

> Troy Magennis. "Software Downloads." Focused Objective. http://focusedobjective.com/software/ (accessed March 20, 2016).

Meadows (2009)

> Donella H. Meadows and Diana Wright. *Thinking in Systems: A Primer*. London: Taylor & Francis.

Reddy (2016)

> Ajay Reddy. *The ScrumBan [R]Evolution: Getting the Most out of Agile, Scrum, and Lean Kanban.* Upper Saddle River, NJ: Addison-Wesley.

Reinertsen (2009)

> Donald G. Reinertsen. *The Principles of Product Development Flow.* Redondo Beach, CA: Celeritas Publishing.

Schwaber (2013)

> Ken Schwaber and Jeff Sutherland. "The Scrum Guide." *Scrum Guides.* http://www.scrumguides.org/scrum-guide.html (accessed January 1, 2016).

Skarin (2015)

> Mattias Skarin. *Real-World Kanban: Do Less, Accomplish More with Lean Thinking.* Frisco, TX: Pragmatic Bookshelf.

Shimokawa (2009)

> Koichi Shimokawa and Takahiro Fujimoto, eds. *The Birth of Lean: Conversations with Taiichi Ohno, Eiji Toyoda, and Other Figures Who Shaped Toyota Management: 1.0.* Cambridge, MA: The Lean Enterprise Institute, Inc.

Shook (2014)

> John Shook and Chet Marchwinski, eds. *Lean Lexicon: A Graphical Glossary for Lean Thinkers*, 5th ed. Cambridge, MA: The Lean Enterprise Institute, Inc.

Steyaert (2014)

> Patrick Steyaert. "Discovery Kanban." Okaloa. http://www.discovery-kanban.com/ (accessed December 11, 2015).

Taleb (2013)

Nassim Nicholas Taleb. *Antifragile: Things That Gain from Disorder*. London: Penguin Books.

Vacanti (2015)

Daniel S. Vacanti. *Actionable Agile Metrics for Predictability: An Introduction*. Victoria, BC: LeanPub.

Weibull (1951)

Waloddi Weibull. "A Statistical Distribution Function of Wide Applicability." *Journal of Applied Mechanics*, 18(3): 293–97.

Wikipedia (2015a)

"Fitness Landscape." *Wikipedia*. https://en.wikipedia.org/wiki/Fitness_landscape (accessed October 30, 2015).

Wikipedia (2015b)

"Monte Carlo Method." *Wikipedia*. https://en.wikipedia.org/wiki/Monte_Carlo_method (accessed December 11, 2015).

Wikipedia (2015c)

"Stationary Process." *Wikipedia*. https://en.wikipedia.org/wiki/Stationary_process (accessed May 27, 2015).

Womack (2003)

James P. Womack and Daniel T. Jones. *Lean Thinking: Banish Waste and Create Wealth in Your Corporation*. London: Simon & Schuster.

Yoshima (2013)

Rodrigo Yoshima. "Management and Change—Avoiding the Rocks." *Lean Kanban North America*, United States: SlideShare. http://www.slideshare.net/rodrigoy/management-and-change-avoidin (accessed April 5, 2016).

Acknowledgements

This book would not have been possible without the many people who have contributed to the development of the Kanban Method over the past 10 years, and those authors and practitioners who pioneered methods that preceded it, and which Kanban draws from and builds on. They are too numerous to mention, but we thank them all.

Our principal reviewers, Mike Burrows, Alexei Zheglov, and Klaus Leopold, made important and helpful contributions that have improved the book's content and—particularly where some changes have been made to familiar concepts in the Method—helped to hone its wording and impact. Contributions from Troy Magennis, Richard Turner, Dan Vacanti, and Larry Maccherone have also been most helpful, along with comments from many reviewers, including Janice Linden-Reed, Irina Dzhambazova, David Denham, John Coleman, Jon Terry, Martien van Steenbergen, Nader Talai, Dan Brown, Daniel Doiron, and Helen Carmichael.

There are many people to thank for help with the actual production of the book—our book editor, Wes Harris, copy editor and designer, Vicki Rowland, and illustrators Jane Pruitt and Eugenia Glas, chief among them.

Finally we are indebted to the worldwide Kanban community who continue to use, challenge, improve and extend this method. This book could not have existed without you.

About the Authors

David J Anderson
@lki_dja, dja@leankanban.com

David J Anderson is an innovator in management thinking for 21st-century businesses. He is CEO of Lean Kanban Inc., a training, consulting, events, and publishing business, making new ideas accessible to managers across the globe. He has more than 30 years' experience in the high-technology industry, starting with games in the early 1980s. He worked at IBM, Sprint, Motorola, and Microsoft, as well as a number of startup businesses. He is the pioneer of both the Kanban Method and Enterprise Services Planning.

David is the author of three books: *Kanban: Successful Evolutionary Change for Your Technology Business*, *Lessons in Agile Management: On the Road to Kanban*, and *Agile Management for Software Engineering: Applying the Theory of Constraints for Business Results*.

Andy Carmichael
@andycarmich

Andy Carmichael is a coach, consultant, and business builder who has been at the forefront of process change in software development teams for many years. His clients include major players in finance, software engineering, utilities, and telecoms—as well as a number of startups and SMEs—all of which share the goals of gaining competitive advantage through increased business agility. He is active in the Kanban and Agile communities and is a Kanban Coaching Professional.

Andy has edited and co-authored three books: *Object Development Methods*, *Developing Business Objects*, and *Better Software Faster*. When not engrossed in technical work, he enjoys singing, golf, and entertaining, particularly when his large grown-up family comes home to visit.

Index

Y

leankanban.com

About Lean Kanban, Inc.

Lean Kanban, Inc. (LKI) is dedicated to developing and promoting the principles and practices of the Kanban Method to achieve the highest quality delivery of professional services through using Kanban. LKI programs include professional development training, a certified training curriculum, events, and published materials.

Certified Kanban Training

Lean Kanban University (LKU) offers a complete curriculum of certified Kanban classes ranging from introductory to advanced, as well as enterprise services. Visit **edu.leankanban.com** to find certified Kanban training or a knowledgeable and experienced coach or trainer in your area. Additionally, Lean Kanban Services offers private training, coaching, and consulting worldwide.

Credentialing Programs

LKU provides leadership training for managers, coaches, and trainers. Professional designations include Team Kanban Practitioner, Kanban Management Professional, Kanban Coaching Professional, and Accredited Kanban Trainer. Certified training helps to raise the level of your Kanban expertise and enables you to earn your professional credential.

Global Conference Series

Join the global Kanban community with Lean Kanban events. The Lean Kanban events series focuses on providing pragmatic, actionable guidance for improving business agility and managing risk with Kanban and related methods. Visit **conf.leankanban.com** for a calendar of upcoming conferences and events.